FROM THE DEVIL'S PULPIT

John Agard was born in Guyana and came to Britain in 1977. He won the Casa de las Americas Prize in 1982 for his *Man to Pan*, and has published two collections with Serpent's Tail, *Mangoes and Bullets* and *Lovelines for a Goat-Born Lady*. His latest book of poems is *From the Devil's Pulpit* (Bloodaxe Books, 1997). He is a popular children's writer whose titles include *Get Back Pimple* (Viking), *Laughter is an Egg* (Puffin), *Grandfather's Old Bruk-a-down Car* (Red Fox), *I Din Do Nothing* (Red Fox), and *We Animals Would Like a Word with You* (Bodley Head), which was shortlisted for the Kurt Maschler Award.

As a touring speaker with the Commonwealth Institute, he visited nearly 2000 schools promoting Caribbean culture and poetry, and has performed on television and around the world. In 1989 he was awarded an Arts Council Bursary and in 1993 became the first Writer in Residence at London's South Bank Centre, who published *A Stone's Throw from Embankment*, a collection written during that residency. He has also written plays. He lives with the poet Grace Nichols and family in Sussex.

Tim + Lizzie

Devilish
good
wishes

JOHN AGARD

John Agard

FROM THE
Keats House

DEVIL'S PULPIT

BLOODAXE BOOKS

ISBN: 1 85224 406 2

First published 1997 by
Bloodaxe Books Ltd,
P.O. Box 1SN,
Newcastle upon Tyne NE99 1SN.

Bloodaxe Books Ltd acknowledges
the financial assistance of Northern Arts.

Cover printing by J. Thomson Colour Printers Ltd, Glasgow.

Printed in Great Britain by
Cromwell Press Ltd, Broughton Gifford, Melksham, Wiltshire.

For Bridget

God is good and the Devil isn't bad either.

IRISH PROVERB

One man's god was his enemy's devil.

BARBARA G. WALKER:
The Women's Encyclopedia of Myths and Secrets

*The Devil is as much a manifestation
of the religious sense as are the gods.*

JEFFREY BURTON RUSSELL: *The Devil*

*In no other religion is there anything comparable in
power and fearful monstrosity to the Christian Devil.*

KAREN ARMSTRONG: *The Gospel according to Woman*

The Devil, it seems, has a million and one disguises.

PETER STANFORD: *The Devil: A Biography*

*The Devil will take your soul and keep it.
I will take your sole and heel it.*

SIGN AT DUBLIN SHOEMENDER'S

*Spell my name backwards.
Ask yourself: Have you LIVED?*

Yours truly, THE DEVIL

Acknowledgements

I would like to thank Eric Bloodaxe for taking the Devil on board his longship; my agent Caroline Sheldon for being very positive about the Devil; Satoshi Kitamura for his devilish drawings; the Hayward Gallery's Inner Eye touring exhibition (curated by Marina Warner) for drawing attention at Brighton Museum to the haunting eye of Redon's *The Temptation of St Anthony*; the Drama House production of *Words from Jerusalem*, devised by Joan Bakewell and broadcast on BBC 1 where 'Lucifer's Canticle for Gethsemane' first appeared; and to you, dear reader, for joining the forked trail.

Contents

Sidekick of God.
Co-partners in time.
Together we deal the cards.
Together we load the dice.
Together we divide the winnings.
Never mind the stakes.
What's the good of grace
without the salt of sin?

Let the Book of Temptation begin.

APPLECALYPSE

Virtue! a fig! 'tis in ourselves that we are thus,
or thus. Our bodies are our gardens, to the which
our wills are gardeners.

SHAKESPEARE: *Othello* (IAGO)

So I keep my womb empty
and full of possibility.

Each month
the blood sheets down
like good rain.

I am the gardener.
Nothing grows without me.

ERICA JONG: *Gardener*

In the Beginning Was...

In a nimbus of blue light
I Lucifer homeward fell –
and the sun sounded its bell
in the temple of my head.

Behind my back, celestial keys
jangled in a shut kingdom
and the harsh harp of hierarchy
howled in my heart's chamber.

Heaven's door had closed its welcome
like the pages of the Good Book.
Forbidding, formal, well-bound.
Branding me a seraphic crook.

An ambitious angelic upstart
who had overstepped the mark
with an urge to outreach the stars
and lend the galaxy my face.

Rumour had it I was too proud –
not one of the cherubic crowd.
But radiance was all I had in common
with those flaming hosts who deemed me demon.

So be it. Here beginneth my testament
with that apple-eating incident.

Applecalypse

I

Eva, mind if I call you Eva?
Have you got something against fruit?
Come on Eva speak the truth.

Have you truly experienced
the absolute yum of plum
the afterglow of avocado
the summery of strawberry
the fleshly figment of fig?

Don't tell me you're allergic
to the mythic munch of pomegranate
the oracular pulp of orange
the glandular grapple
with a simple apple.

A veritable juice downpour
in the valley of the throat.
And if I may misquote:
'An apple a day keeps the devil away.'

II

If all that apple spiel
doesn't make you feel
to tongue steal
and unpeel
the little orb
shining as anything
from the harvest
of Hesperides

If all that apple hype
doesn't make you a ripe
target for marketing –
a prime sampler
of the puckered product –
and it won't cost a buck
today you're in luck

Then answer me truly –
when again will you get this chance
to combine Vitamin C
with a thirst for ecstasy?

III

Such a difficult customer, this Eva.
I wonder what makes her waver –
so irresistible, when irresolute,
I for one would certainly crave her
if I were dissolute.
But she knows me better than anyone.
She's already seen through my snakesuit.

My God, she's testing my powers to ad lib.
All right Eva, I take what you say
about this business of the rib:
that the whole thing was rigged.
Of course it was your arching bone
– nothing to do with the Most High throne –
and with a little help from a hissing word,
that launched Adam on his way
from that nondescript bed of clay.
Now he's off naming, blissful as a bird.
Sometimes I get the urge to rib him.
But we'll keep that our little secret.

Anyway, back to the business of fruit.
Let's get down to taking temptation by the root.

Come on Eva.
Try a half.
Between us
we could write
an epitaph
to the forbidden.

Bite.

IV

And after she had bitten
her face was burdened
with a glow most sweet

14

And all that first man
back from a bout of naming
could say was 'Helpmeet

There'll be trouble from above.'
For he who had given names
to creeping thing and flying form

Had stumbled on no word for Love.

V

And even as his teeth were sunk into the apple globe
he felt for a split second at the crossroads.
Part of him succoured by the unnamed juice
Part of him fearing the sword of Justice.

Well Adam, boy, allow me to say
you've come a long way from anonymous clay.
Knowledge is beginning to open its door.
So bite on. Explore the cavern of the core.

But expect some retribution from the Big Chief
That Sovereign of the straight and narrow path.
So I'll be as brief as the famous fig leaf
that will adorn the altar of your private parts.

Helpmeet. Is that all you could call your better half?
She who weaned you to the wisdom of the grass
and succumbed to the secrets of the stars.
Adam, believe me, Eva knows where it's at.

Never mind that flaming advocate of wrath
Who will call your rapture insolence.
What's Eden after all but a den of innocence.
Remember, nothing ventured, nothing gained.

Think of all the sunlight and the rain
that goes into the grooming of a single apple.
If my argument seems serpentine and subtle
How accept the pleasure without the pain

Turn your back on Eden for the endlessly possible
See temptation as bounteous benediction.
As for original sin? A clear misnomer.
A chincanery of words. A sleight of tongue.

That stirring of limb for limb and skin for skin
Is not exactly what I would call sin.
That ancient urge to bridge the solitary abyss.
Come on you two. Go for it. The first kiss.

VI

And so the mouth held forth its promise
like a baboon's pleasurable pouch noticed
for the first time, signalling another path
crooked and wide as temptation,
shedding in a split second its innocent tongue
for one only the gospel of flesh could fathom.

And he whose mouth was given to naming
was suddenly silenced by the un-utterable
And she to whom apocalypse was apple
trusted in the testament of the moment
since eternity was void of sound and scent.
Thus the tongue exalted in its own oracle.

And how I hissed to the beat of Revelation
and gloried in the frailty of right and wrong.

VII

The first unrecorded kiss.
Then Eden thrust its pelvis
in the face of you know who.

And who'll blame those original two
for wanting to try out their tongue
when a noun was a beautiful bliss.

So I'll tread with them
the cobble stones of temptation.
But I'll lift their feet towards the horizon

even as they stumbled, my frail ones.

VIII

Only the serpent in the dust
Wriggling and crawling,
Grinned an evil grin and thrust
His tongue out with its fork.
          CHRISTINA ROSSETTI: *Eve*

No, Christina, I did not grin an evil grin.
In fact I wished them luck in their new enterprise
pleased with myself for having opened their eyes
to the limitations of Paradise.

No one in their right mind would suggest
that this pair had just commited original sin
so wondrous the sun shone
in the sanctuary of their skin
and what was done could not be undone.
If you looked keenly you'd detect a certain glow
as if guilt had wrapped them in its subtle bloom.
But there was no room for regret
or ruminations on the pros and cons of sin.
Adam had a sheepish schoolboy sort of grin
as if he had braved the headmaster's cane
and secretly would do the same again.
Besides, he could always pass the blame
and say she talked him into it.
But my God, how he'd miss assembling
those animals and giving each a name.
If they could counsel him now, would fowl and beast
pity his mortal trembling?

Eva meanwhile picked a myrtle sprig
and made it into the first ribbon
So Eden lingered in her hair.
And in the final moment of their parting
she thought she saw the serpent raise
the formidable flower of his eye
and she knew that look
would be companion to her solitary days
like a perfumed petal pressed between a book.

Towards New Doors

I

Farewell Eden. Welcome sweat of brow.
No more those paradaisical gates.
Walk hand in hand towards your hates
and of course your loves, and the plough
that needs must plead with unyielding earth.

See, the rainbow of temptation
strokes your solitude. New doors
open their horizons. Walk on.

II

What manner of children will you spawn
when the dawn of history delivers its demons?

Already murder has marked one of your sons
and pain will multiply your daughters' conception.

Even the ground opens its mouth to receive you
and the very stones prepare their sermons.

But for hell's sake don't get nostalgic
or start falling for that divine trick.

Simply give thanks to temptation
that sharpens the blade of the knife
and sweetens the taste of life

Remember, without me you'd still be
in a fools' paradise –
eyes unopened to the rapture of risk.

Lucifer as Pristine Instigator of Workers' Rights

It must be difficult to guard the gates of Paradise
when sleep marches in your eyes
and you'd rather lay down your flaming sword
to take a fag or five. The signs
are you're overworked and bored
for eternity is one unending shift.
You wish you could complain to the Lord
or put in a claim for overtime.
But the last thing you want is to start a rift
in employer-employee relationship
though a breakdown is aeons overdue.
Then a little voice says right out of the blue,
Look here, you sword-waving, grim-faced cherubims,
it's all well and good guarding the Tree of Life
but Progress you know springs from the seeds of strife.

Funny how a word in the left ear at the right time
can unsettle a hierarchy. Thanks to me.

Gift of Tears

Paradise was all smiles

the stones giggled
at the purity
of a river's jokes

the birds tittered
with their feathers
over their lips

the sun grinned
till its yellow cheeks
were all splinters

the streams spilled
into uncontrollable fits
because the fish tickled

the wind chuckled
the flowers winked
the leaves were in hysterics

the omnipresent sky split
into outbursts
of cosmic laughter.

It was all too much.
I just had to step in
and wipe away Eden's grin.

Prepare the first couple
for the ache to follow.
Wise them up to trouble.

Bring the gift of tears
that would cleanse sorrow
when eyes are burdened fruit.

THE DEVIL LEADS
A BUSY SOCIAL LIFE

*Better keep the devil at the door
than turn him out of the house.*

SCOTTISH PROVERB

On First Name Terms

Hey. None of this Beelzebub business.
Lighten up. No more Prince of Darkness
and all that Devil's Advocate
kind of stuff. I'm your mate.
It's all right to call me Dev
and I'll call you Les or Mags or Trev.
Formality stinks. Don't say evil. Say Ev.

Lucifer the Perfect Host

I

Whom did you expect to answer the doorbell?
A horned host in flaming robes of hell?

My cigarette holder is my only trident
and cloven feet were never my bent.

II

It's good to be entertained by moonlight
when the angel of darkness puts on her tights

and offers you a bowl of forbidden fruit.
That's how she separates the boy from the brute.

III

Please accept my apology, dear guest,
If I'm not the fiend you were led to expect.

Make yourself at home and do as you wish.
I'll put on my mask and bring out the swish.

IV

Do let me take your coat and your conscience.
I will hang them both by the entrance.

Sorry about my directions. I did say
bear right till you come to the brimstone driveway.

V

Vegetarian? Then avoid the goat stew.
But may I tempt you with a brew

of my special bifurcated root with cheese
I picked up duty-free in Hades.

O, the one in the hat, she's Tiamat. Stunning.
And the good fellow beside her is Robin.

Now that we've all been introduced,
why not mingle, hang loose, be seduced.

House-Warming

Open your heart
and I will give you
the key to hell.
No need to knock
or ring the bell.
Just let yourself in.
Make yourself at home
like a toad
under a rock.
A wart on a skin.

Dial the Devil

Taking the side of flesh and bone
the Devil will not install
a dreaded answer-phone.

Day and night, the Devil is all
for the person-to-person call.
The dance of the nuance.
The slithering shifts of tone
that make for Humanspeak.
None of that abysmal
disembodied BEEP.

Old Horny's voice of velvet
will even accept Collect.

Ars Conversationis

The Devil is an excellent conversationalist
who speaks in parenthesis –
who scatters the spoor of commas
where pauses may or may not matter –
who breaks the bread of repartee
to grace a situation's gravity –
who drops the occasional remark
that dispels the listener into the dark
where all contradictions unite –
But being a good listener, well informed, polite,
the Devil will never put you on the spot
by asking *Have you seen the light or not?*

Of Course the Devil Speaks Latin

Membrum genitale
Pudendum muliebre
Fellatio in flagrante
Cunnilingus uninterruptus
O conjugation unctuous
if you'll excuse my latin.

Goat on the Catwalk

Ever seen a goat
in a fur coat?
Well, here I come folks –
to strut the catwalk
with clovenfoot grace –
a role model
in diabolical lace.

Tell the Vatican
I'll be in Milan
en route to Paris
next stop London New York –
every fashion capital
will see me stride colossal.
In case you didn't know
I'm also big in Tokyo.

Prepare the paparazzi
and the likes of Armani
for a satanic surprise.
I've dropped my anorexic guise.
All will be revealed
in the fleshly fullness of time.
And heaven help the catwalks of the world
(for better or for worse)
when I expose the cherubic globes
of my lower universe.

Reservation for Two

I

Waiter, bring me a bottle
of your best Baudelairean wine
(opened with the Devil's corkscrew).
Tonight I feel like a vintage swine.

II

Book me a room with a view
in the London Hilton.
I'm having a naughty weekend
with the shadow Minister Milton.

III

Reserve a table for two
in your most nookie corner.
I'm in the mood for five-star food
and talk enlightening and lewd.

IV

Serenade me with harps and horns
and a sonata by Tartini.
Tell the candle at both ends
to burn O so slowly.

In Keeping With R.S.V.P. Protocol, the Devil Cordially Responds to a Costume Party Invite

Shall I come as a he?
Shall I come as a she?
How shall I bedeck me?
O decisions decisions.

Shall I come with feathered wing
of a fallen celestial?
Or shall I slip into something
a little more bestial?

Maybe my Goat-labelled number,
designed when horns were all the rage?
Or shall I wear my Ass's mask
complete with rampant appendage?

Maybe a skirt of serpent skin
set off with forked accessory?
Or shall I don the livery
of a lying attorney?

Shall I come costumed
as God's articulate Ape?
Or shall I assume
a more teasing shape?

A G-stringed angel aglow
with a bulbous halo?
Or shall I strut my Siren dress
to lure you to the naked test?

Shall I drape the robe of Vicar
above my ordained knickers?
Or shall I act the Buffoon
in a protuberant pantaloon?

How do I make up my mind
when one's wardrobe flaunts such a line
of motley pedigree?
Ah, the life of a V.I.P.

But since my presence will be missed,
I'll simply come as The Other,
so when the party's fully pissed
I'll play the Scapegoat, brother,

for all the insults that you hiss.

The Devil at Lords

There was nothing in the match.
A tame predictable draw.
A wicket without promise.
Till the Devil in inspired fit
did a lightning streak across the pitch.
A copper's helmet covering
a bifurcated prick
but unable to contain
two Beelzebub tits
swinging their googlies
with glorious certainty.
Such unorthodox phenomenon
made W.G. Grace turn in his grave.
Dicky Bird attempted flight.
Nothing in the rule book
said androgynous demons
were not the life and soul of cricket.

Watch it, Luther, There's an Uncatered for Caterpillar on Your Plate

'Tis an an emblem of the devil in its crawling walk,
and bears his colours in its changing hue.
LUTHER'S *Table-Talk*

Note the crawling skin.
The Satanic wriggler
in hairy form.
Of demon born
is the caterpillar
and lacks table manners.

Not so fast, Luther.
Must I reform
your catechismic eye
to see the crawling one
audaciously transformed
to pious butterfly.

The Devil Passes the Pet Shop

I'd rather comb a goat's beard by moonlight,
than clean a hamster's cage all filled with shite.

The Seeds of Wimbledon

Women seeds and men seeds
come together in strawberry June
to inherit the kingdom of Wimbledon
where the seeded mingle with the unseeded
and the grass is green with summer light
and some seeds fall to the left
and some seeds fall to the right
and some seeds fall on good ground
and some seeds are gone with the wind
and some seeds are hairy some seeds are smooth
and some seeds take root
and some seeds bear fruit
and that is the bleeding unceded

truth

Carnival of the Alps

Cloven feet were made equally
for carnival as for skiing –
the downward pull of ecstasy
not altogether unfamiliar.
Even falling on one's fundament
in an Alpine element
somehow brought back memories
of an avalanche of angels –
that long-ago apocalyptic fall.

And a halo of sounds reeking of carnival
drifted from the ice-bearded mountains,
as the Devil, seal-walking on skis
among the clouds' principalities,
arrived at the conclusion that everywhere
the rich and poor put on a costume
to outwit the solitary peaks of doom.

And falling for the third time
on a cross of skis
among a cathedral of glaciers –
the horned one prayed
for the human casualities
of life's sloping masquerade.

Captain Lucifer Speaking

Ladies and Gentlemen,
this is Captain Lucifer speaking.
We're now cruising at low altitude
over the springs of Hades.
Fasten your seat belts. Please.

You may experience turbulence
and apocalypse below the waist.

Observe the way the stewardess
will undress
in the best possible taste
and do the unspeakable with the oxygen mask.

Passengers requiring duty-free dildos
and bifurcated condoms
will be given the opportunity to do so.

My co-pilot and I will shortly be coming
down the aisle
and exposing ourselves.
A spot of exhibitionism will prepare your minds

for the descent.

In case you're wondering who's flying

the controls are at the mercy of God.

I repeat. The controls...

A Light Traveller

The Devil always travels light
and never suffers from jet lag.
A toothbrush like a small trident
in an overnight bag.
A copy of Dostoyevsky
for a little light reading.
A change of underwear.
Nothing unnecessary.
Nothing, as they say, to declare
except a duty-free conscience
and a passport that never expires.

WHERE THE PATH FORKS

The blackest humour is the lifeblood of the brightest genesis.

WILSON HARRIS: *Genesis of the Clowns*

Evil travels in straight lines.

AFRICAN SAYING

Where the Path Forks

Cain
Cain

run from
your conscience

The dying
light
of your brother's face
has become the wolf
that devours your sleep

Cain
Cain

run from
your conscience

The stabbing
knife
that bears your name
is lying where the sheep
have newly lain

Cain
Cain

run from
your conscience

Where the path forks
there you'll find a friend

By Their Fruits You Shall Know Them

What fruit did Hitler eat? Or Stalin?
Or we ourselves who used that murderous
miracle at Hiroshima.
ARCHIBALD MacLEISH

See, an ordinary man reaching toward a bowl.
Even his moustache anticipates the aroma
of an apricot, a peach, or I daresay, an apple.

No subtle serpent lies hidden in its core.
Only fragrant fruit in simple porcelain
adorning his mother's dining-table.

So let psychiatrists unearth some childhood trauma
or some perversion of the brain to explain
the forked path of murder or miracle.

I've said it before and I'll say it again:
Each heart sows the seeds of its own Satan.
This simple truth makes it possible

for a man to shine an apple on his sleeve
while contemplating the extinction of millions.

Lucifer's Lullaby

How innocent are you, little babe
in your Moses basket,
peaceful as the vampire asleep
in his box of native soil?
Not yet for you the trouble and toil
of workaday pen or plough
and who would brand as fallen
the angel that lays upon your brow?

How innocent are you, little babe
wrapped in slumber's cloth.
Your fragrant skin cries out to be kissed
and as yet no knife glints
in the tiny flower of your fist.
And who'd guess this dream-filled basket
would be your first station to the dock
and murder become your halo?

Alas, my little innocent,
the forked path creepeth to your door.
A mother longs to turn back the clock
and weepeth for the apple of her eye.
Lamentation is all her being
while experts dwell on the 'criminal gene'
and invoke the social wrongs and woes.

But as the poet
sees the worm inside the rose,
beneath love's cooing lullaby
I hear also hate's cradling hiss.
O little babe, blessed only with
the stigma of a mother's kiss.

Prodigy

That ordinary woman
who wheeled an infant's corpse
in an ordinary pram.
Hanged in her wedding-dress
and laid to rest
among the damned.
Did she nurture
some genetic curse?
Show me the serpent
hidden in her purse.

That serial killer
with the freshman looks
who tended dying creatures
like a Francis of Assisi.
That silent rapist
who devoured books
and surprised the social worker
with quotations from Shelley.
Is it written in the news
there are cloven feet
inside his shoes?

Give to evil any face you choose.
Spare not any sex or race
its icons and its demons.
Demand of history its vile prodigy.

Lucifer's Obituary to Judas

The rope has left its radiant halo
around the neck of Judas.
Was it a juniper or a cedar alas
   that suspended his body's sad tarot
for the vultures to make their chariot?
O juniper that gave foundation
   to the temple of Solomon
O cedar fragrant as the limbs of Lebanon
   What final branch of refuge for this lost son
whose intentions were less precise
   than thirty pieces of silver?
Which dove of solace will perch upon those eyes?
For your garments, dear Iscariot,
   Who will cast a solitary lot
Or balm your limbs in fabled spices?
Yet, for while, you walked the straight and narrow
   and gloried in Nazareth's numinous glow
till you stumbled against temptation.

Little did you know it was all divinely planned.
Brother, sleep well, let me be first to kiss your hand

All Yours to Exorcise

I

Easy to lay your inner demons at the devil's door
and conjoin evil's cause to the name of Eve
who grieved her outcast days for a murdered son
and listened for the footsteps of his vagabond
brother, both nurtured from the same bosom.
What if the devil's door adjoined your heart's portal?
What if yours was the gargoyle grin on a cathedral?

II

And so it was when I rode into the white
darkness, saddling the shoulders of night.
A grotesque icon of your imagination.

Prince of darkness you branded me. Overlord
of an underworld of bitter cold or bitter heat.
Horned one who surveys his kingdom on hoofed feet.

Your inner fears gave darkness a bad press
and your intellect schemed a vile trade
in humans whose skin was the colour of earth.

You smeared the left hand sinister as nakedness,
and untold women who made a covenant
with the inner voice, you smothered at the stake

as if the all-seeing eye of the cunt
threatened you with your own mortality
and blinded you to the words of one crucified.

If I said I am the misconstrued echo
of his words, the duenna shadow of his halo,
you'd most likely look at me as if I lied.

Well then folks I'm all yours to exorcise.

The Enemy Within

Sprinkle my image with water
Scourge my name with salt

I'll play the ready scapegoat
to save you from your fault

Mangle my reflection
in man-made mirror

Pray I flee in terror
from my own dread-filling looks

Tackle me with incantations
and prayers from holy books

Shackle my person in seven loaves
and hope I lose my power

Place your faith in perfumed smoke
at the appointed hour

I'll have the final joke
Your faithful counsellor in sin

Which is just another name
for the enemy within

Colour of Evil

What is the colour of evil I asked of Yellow
who led me past Wordsworth's daffodils and Van Gogh's sunflowers
till we came to flashbacks of Vietnam
where the sun's rays were yellow robes of mourning.

What is the colour of evil I asked of Green
who showed me the springtime hills that held a child's scream
and the grass lost its innocence
to the god of forensic evidence.

What is the colour of evil I asked of Brown
who spoke of the romance of autumn leaves
but I saw baked earth writing its own epitaph
and empty bowls reaching for the world's charity.

What is the colour of evil I asked of Red
who said blood speaks your language as well as mine
but take comfort from the rose
and the anonymous heart of a Valentine.

What is the colour of evil I asked of Blue
who led me through the archives of the skies
where birds of death fashioned by the hands of men
circled in the dazzling air.

What is the colour of evil I asked of Black
who guided me through galleries and museums
where the dark was equated with the beast of fear.
Then stepping through doorways of ancient lore I found darkest

chaos was a mothering force that sat upon a brood of stars.

What is the colour of evil I asked of White
who walked with me across the fugitive snow
that covered a city's scars
under an angelic apron. So I walked on in the light.

And grinned to see the pureness of a page reflecting
my own chameleon grin.

O Ye of Little Faith

Cast bread
to water.

Brown, white,
sliced, whole.

It will return
a thousandfold.

Change a stone
to a croissant.

Feed five thousand
with five loaves
and five fish.

Such holy mathematics
will impress
a multitude.

But it will take
more than a miracle
for them to learn

the lesson of gratitude.

On the Devil's Couch

Get thee behind me
Messrs Freud and Jung.
My couch is for acting the clown.

Unfix your fixation.
Take the lid off your id.
Hang-up your hang-ups.
Crack your hard-boiled ego.

I'll make a shrink of your shadow.

In the Name of Country

If only you could wear
these mountains
as medals on your chest.

If only the rivers
could be impressed
with a hero's homecoming.

If only you could teach
the birds to sing
a national anthem

for one who killed
in the name of country.
Is this too much to ask?

That the trees
would salute
your steps?

That the stones
would stand
to attention?

That the grass
would wave
a small trembling flag

or at the very least
return your lost
soul?

Twins

To bring forth one
is to be blessed.

To bring forth two
is to be twice blessed.

But to bring forth
one black one white

twinned in the same womb
where day and night are one

(now here's a fine kettle
of genetic fish).

That is to enthrone
the miraculous mischief

of ovum and sperm
made flesh and bone.

That is to relearn
the lesson of the Ark –

raven and dove released
from love's tremulous flood.

Second Coming

I

To the beat of Sanctus bells
I will sing the birth

of cherubs with cheeks of Europe
and the forehead of Africa

Paint me, Michelangelo,
an angel named Mulatto

and I will build a covenant
to a mingled Magnificat.

II

Ram-bam-
tam-pam
ring the bells
of Notre Dame
for the coming of Josephine Baker
is at hand.

III

Not light enough for the all-Light.
Not black enough for the all-Black.
What do you do? Bribe the raven and the dove?
Or start a rainbow tribe in the name of love?

The Map of Your Shadow

Gaze, if you dare
into the crystal
ball of darkness
for your figments of fear.

Sink into your pillow's
unfathomable depths
where dreams scatter
their wayward tribes.

Enter the dark continent
you nightly inherit
and fragments of a lost tongue
will extend their welcome.

Follow, stranded angel,
the map of your shadow,
and blackness will unburden
your yoke of light.

Prepare, Prospero,
for Caliban's flight.

Pact

She thinks thunder
and the sky roars.

She thinks drought
and the soil sizzles.

She thinks rust
and weapons blunt.

She thinks storm
and the heavens howl.

She thinks lightning
and the mirror shatters.

She thinks blood
and an Empire falters.

For this, they will bridle her tongue,
and if need be, burn her like the rest

before she thinks love
and infects them all with wholeness.

LEAD US INTO TEMPTATION

I generally avoid temptation
unless I can't resist it.

MAE WEST

The saints (those who are nearly saints) are
more exposed than others to the devil because
the real knowledge they have of their wretchedness
makes the light almost intolerable...

SIMONE WEIL

Lucifer's Canticle for Gethsemane

I

In the Garden of Gethsemane –
there where the olives are pressed
I will put him to his hardest test.

Three temptations I have given
and thrice the man hath shamed me
by resisting every one.

Refusing to turn stones to bread
or make a flying leap of faith.
This fisher of men would not bite the bait.

Not for all the kingdom's glory
would he fall down and worship me
Get thee hence Satan for it is written

But if I am ridded of so easily
how would Eden's apple be bitten
or Gethsemane become a chapter in his story

As well as mine.

II

Tonight in Gethsemane
let uncertainty
be his halo.

Let him kneel
at the crossroads
of yes and no.

Let his mission
find uneven keel
in the anguished waters of doubt.

Let indecision
be his demon
and in his heart fear blossom.

Let him call upon
his heavenly father
to take away the cup

of ordained suffering.
Let a moment's wavering
weaken his resolve.

In a moonlit olive grove
let the juice of this man's love
be accounted for in blood.

III

And when his heart was exceeding sorrowful
Who would tarry with him but one hour? One.
Not Peter. Not James. Not John.
'Couldest not thou watch one hour?'

And I who had fallen from the grace of his eye
Watch each bleeding second furrow his face.
Innocence soon to be ensnared with a kiss.
The sheep scattered. The shepherd smitten.

No doubt he'd say 'for it is written'
and follow his cross-calling to Golgotha.
Become a dove crucified upon a hill.
Very well. Let prophecy be fulfilled.

But one hour is agony to endure
even,for one born for a halo of thorns.
He whose face is balming as the oil of olive.
He who taught to befriend a foe and forgive.

All I wanted was for him to survive
as beautiful. Open to temptation. A mothers son.
I did not want the rapture of his face gone.
I did not want the bread of his body pierced.

Believe me, even this man's garments will not go unsung.

Unicorn at the Lap of Hildegard

Go, unicorn,
demon of the darling horn.
Lay your phallic third eye
at the lap of Hildegard –
Abbess of the Rhine.
She who dealt in sibylline
prophecies and recipes
could have been burnt
for being ahead of her time.

For according to this good nun
the cooperation
of God and the Devil
are necessary for conception.

Angel-ovum demon-sperm?
Angel-sperm demon-ovum?
O miracle of tiny hands
beating the blood-drum.
O miracle of closed eyes
scanning the colour spectrum.

Go, unicorn,
chant an antiphon to the newborn.
Lay your devilish diadem
at the lap of one
who saw Christ's wounds
to jewels transformed.

Almost

Almost was written on your face
where temptation had left its trace.
You almost said No. Almost.

If Only echoed from your cheek.
The spirit willing, the flesh weak.
Things might have been different If Only.

What If left a note in your eyes
because guilt sent out its spies.
If Only What If Was Almost.

Warning All Ascetics

There are devils
in the lentils.

Go On Pandora

What's a box for
if not to be opened?
What's temptation for
if no one succumbs?
A box becomes news
when someone like you
looks inside for clues
to the universe.
Call it a blessing.
Call it a curse.
No more guessing.
Go on Pandora
my enquiring daughter.
Remove the lid
of your curious Grail.
Hope will not fail.

Ride On Lady G

What's the good of riding
in naked glory
through the streets of a town
if you can't catch
the public eye?
No crowd standing by
to urge you on, sister.
No photographer
from the local press
to record your protest.
Not even a snap
for the family album
so your grandchildren
can see Gran's bum
beside a horse's.
Unless, of course,
one breaks the promise
of barred doors
and drawn curtains.
That's where I come in.
Know what I mean Lady G?
Peep he will peep he won't.
Temptation says try.
And so a tailor's eye
is immortalised
and your posterior rides
in the face of posterity.

Lucifer's Epitaph for Lot's Wife

*But his wife looked back from behind him,
and she became a pillar of salt.*
GENESIS 19. 26

HERE STANDS A CRYSTAL MONUMENT
THAT ONCE ANSWERED TO LOT'S WIFE.
A REMINDER THAT TEMPTATION
IS THE VERY SALT OF LIFE.

The Man Who Walked on While
His Wife Became a Pillar of Salt

So you walked on resigned to your lot
cuckolded by a pillar of salt.
Surely your heart harboured a flame
for this woman who answered to your name.
Surely your loins were not past longing
for her who had borne you two daughters.

How the salt hills sparkled in her hair
and the sea's grain garnished her beauty.
How the very winds covered her in crystals
like a shroud of diamonds.
No rain now can wash away
this daughter of Sodom
who gazes backwards rock-still and eternal.

So you walked on infirm but firm
in the singleness of your stride.
Not once heeding the little voice inside
– the weevil among the wheat of your thoughts.
Keeping your mind fixed on the city ahead
not once turning towards your scattered cattle,
kinsmen or the one who had shared your bed
and made bearable these forbidding hills.

You triumphed in the tyranny of will
or at least for a while you thought you did.
No, my friend, you won't escape so easily.
There in a cave overlooking the very salt sea
your daughters will enter your drunken sleep
with the softness of a harlot.
O son of Haran, weep for your Lot.

Lucifer to Icarus

Icarus even before you flew
I could have told you a thing or two.

Beware the singeing sunlight
that will unwax your flight

And ground your feathered aspiration.
Remind you that you're after all a craftsman's son

Not a god who dwells on pedestals of clouds
or hobnobs with that seraphic crowd.

A simple boy who thought the runway of the sky
was space enough for his Concorde heart

thought he'd fly into the sun's signalling eye.
Dare the evanescent tarmac of god-given air.

Darling boy, I could have told you beware
of the treacherous purity of the blinding light

yet even as you obeyed the downward call of destiny
you would not make a god of gravity.

Freedom was the name of the demon
that gave you faith and drove you on

though some would argue curiosity
or simply say too damn stubborn.

But if deafness to Father was your fatal
Sin, I relived with you the Passion of my Fall.

For I was the little voice that said you can do it.
Be tempted to defy the tyranny of the sun.

To be frank, I knew you'd never make it.
Yet how my heart felt pierced with a sword

when your lovely body drowned. O my rebel son.

The Risen and the Fallen

With earth I made my tryst
when the morning star of my body
greeted ground. Another abyss.

It was good to be free of feathers.
My shoulders lost their primal tail.
Ready for the wheel. Unfettered.

It was then my earth-blessed eyes
witnessed the first shifting miracle.
A solitary feather transformed

into full flutter of a crowing Cock.
The one who is morning's oracle.
Trumpeter of the Fallen

Lucifer and Risen Christ.

A Short Romp Among Saints

I *Absolution or Ablution?*

Cleanliness, I hear you say
is next to godliness.

Are you sure?

For I have seen the saintly
haloed in their own mess –

they who venerated their sores
as faith confirmed –

crawled on all fours
and revelled in vermin –

and considered a bath
an invitation to sin.

Does this mean
that the straight and narrow path

never leads to a sauna?

Such thoughts I ponder
under the shower.

II *St Augustine*

Take a deep theological breath
before you confess, St Augustine.
I'm not talking incontinence and sin.
I'm onto the business of breaking wind,
or to put it bluntly – 'farting'.
Let's face it. There are farters and farters.
You have your tentative breeze-teaser,
and you have your full-blown olympian gale-blower.
So let's take a backward glance
at these masters of the art
of backdoor orchestration.

That Egyptian courtier for a start
whose bowels 'sang like a harp',
especially after a banquet of beans.
That English landsman of medieval means
who curry favoured the King's presence
with a fife of flatulence.
That French music hall maestro of the rude sound –
wasn't he toasted for bringing the house down
with controlled cannonades from the bum?
And what about Salvador Dali?
Didn't he wax with long-winded spirituum
on this most unsurrealistic act,
which is supposed to scare off a demon?
It's not for me to go on ad infinitum.

But it took a saint like you, St Augustine,
to describe the deed with just the right words:
'There are those that can break wind backwards
so artfully you would think they sang.'
Come on, Gustie, confess it's the truth.
And you said it in Latin to boot.

III *St George and the Dragon*

Who will lance
the Dragon?
Who will teach
the flaming one
the dance
of death?

Who will face
its breath
with a
patriarch's
stance?

Why you, St George
And by George
I'll be damned

But there's fire coming out of your mouth!

IV *St Theresa of Avila*

A penny for your thoughts,
St Theresa of Avila –
I almost said of Vanilla,
knowing that sweet tooth of yours
for the divine preserve
of quince and Easter cake.
Oh, it wasn't against your Credo
to compare a Seville patio
to slabs of iced sugar. I like that.

And to wear a woollen tunic
in summer's roasting heat,
you'd be the first to agree
was a rather penitential feat.
An inquisition of the body-part.

You're a woman after my own heart.
'Preserve us from sullen saints,'
you said. I couldn't agree more.
That's why I came knocking at your door.
I didn't mean for you to faint.
For you, I'd have done anything.
Run bubble bath. Even paint
your toes or massage your skin.

What made you call me, and I quote,
'That poor wretch who cannot love'?
Somehow, you haven't got me quite sussed.
For when the holy word goosed
your swooning throat,
I thought to myself, if such rapture
be a mystical perk,
then let love do its ensnaring work
and be my wretched capture.

v *St Michael*

It's a tricky business –
this weighing of souls,
especially when demons
are doing their best to tip
the delicate balance.
But somebody's got to do it.

And who dares question the fairness
of your archangelic metrics
that leave everything to chance?
But what I'd like to know, St Michael,
which weighs more, sunrise or nightfall?
A fallen feather or petal?
How does a halo
compare with a shadow –
I mean, kilo for kilo?
How do you measure in a scale-pan
the soul of a woman and a man?

I don't envy you, St Michael.
No greengrocer would go for your job,
even for a few extra bob.

vi *St Bridget*

St Bridget
whose footsteps blessed
the shamrock's trinity –

associate
of blacksmithery and poetry.
Druid's fair daughter

baptised
by none other than the Patriarch.
Did your mammy never tell thee

that whistling
was the domain of farmers and tarts?

Yet, good lady of Kildare,
your whistling struck
a keening note in Ireland's heart,

and it came to be
that many a wanton daughter
was fondly christened Biddy.

VII *St John the Baptist and Salomé*

Come in from the wilderness
O St John the Baptist.
Just think what you've missed.
You could have settled down
with Salomé's saucy dish
in homely coupledom.
Instead, you settled for wild locust
and a sackcloth epitaph.
Never baptised your staff
in the water of her font.
All she wanted was to mount
the ladder
of your limbs.
But the only head you gave her
was on a silver platter.
By then it didn't matter.
Alas, O hairy messenger,
she could have veiled
you in seven veils
and bid you live
to tell the tale.

THE CARNAL HUBBUB

All flesh is trouble.

EDWARD DAHLBERG

Battle of the Buttocks

I

Blessed are the meek.
If someone smites you
on the left buttock,
turn the other cheek.

II

Rumour has it
I have no buttocks.
Beautiful in front.
Hollow at the back.
No comment.
I'll let that pass.
Or must I expose
my golden ass?

III

Thou art Venus Kallipygos.
And upon this rock
I will build your buttock.

IV

Hotfoot
they came from far and wide
to stare upon the bot
of Venus Hottentot.

She who spent
her final days
in a chamber of glass.

Burnt on the stake
of Europe's gaze.
Guillotined by eyes.
O what have they learnt
from the last of the tribe?

V

Lay down weapons.
Bare all buttocks.
Only the slaughtered
on the bleeding sand
will not tell the tale
of this fleshly fanfare
of surrender.

Get Down Ye Angels

Get down ye angels from the heights.
Try a few of earth's numinous delights:
the orgiastic rustling of the grass.
The wind's brazen feather tickling your arse.

Exchange your robe even for a day
with the raiment of one made of clay.
Lay down your harp and dig these pipes I play.

I'll put my lips to the weeping reeds
till temptation thrills the heart of every hill
and the very stones begin the dance of leaves
as if stones had gained a fluttering will.

Welcome ye cherubs to the carnal hubbub.
Take a break from heaven's eternal monotone.
Inhabit the splendid risk of flesh and bone.

The Devil at Carnival

The Devil playing mas
The Devil pinching ass
So if you ain't feeling carnal
better keep away from carnival

Blow the horn ring the bell
Beelzebub in a pleated gown
prancing through the town
sidestepping holy water
to a beat of iron

Blow the horn ring the bell
The language of the infidel
Whose language? Whose infidel?
Whose heaven? Whose hell?
Beelzebub brandish your tongue

Holy be the cassock and habit
Say holier be the cock and slit
And so the Devil dress up in satin
talking a string of Latin

Genitalia bacchanalia inter alia
Arses amores galore
Is best to pray on all fours
when pleasure knock answer the door

Conjugate your intentions
I declare my declensions
Show me your vocative
I show you my accusative

Blow the horn ring the bell
Bring on the angel Jezebel
Incubus and Succubus
costumed to the crotch
gyrating in flagrante
like something out of Dante

The Senate can legislate
but can't control the floodgate
Go and tell the Prime Minister
Pudenda and member on the agenda
Delirium dwelling in the drum
fire fire in the sanctum

He-jab-jab she-jab-jab whipcrack
strike ground wine down low
gloria in excelsis libido
back-to-back belly-to-belly
vox populi vox populi whistle-blow

Blood is boss on the Cross
but on bum-bum jam-jam day
volupte carne holding sway
and Lucifer in a crown of horns
waving the key to the kingdom
where the sheep lieth down with the goat
hosanna hosanna to the lowest of the low.

All Things Cloven and Horned

All things cloven and horned
    as bright and beautiful to me
    as Creation's first magnificent morn

I have nothing against creeping form
    for blessèd be the slime

I speak no ill of things that fly
    for holy be the sky

1 have no quarrel with scale or fin
    for welcome be the water

But I admit a soft spot
    for the cloven and the horned

Greetings O Goat my favoured one

In my heart I hold dear your bearded light
I bless you there on your biblical height.

Glory Glory Be to Chocolate

Food cravings are not a sign of weakness; they are a sign
of biological advancement. They really are Eve's blessing.
            DEBRAH WATERHOUSE: *Why Women Need Chocolate*

NAUGHTY BUT NICE

(Note the phrase minted
by the author of *The Satanic Verses*)

So I say it twice
glory glory be to chocolate
in all its manifestations –

Mouth-watering bars
of butterscotch and caramel
that ring the tastebud bells

Brownies candies cookies
Cinnamon-flavoured little imps
that twinkle at the tongue.

O sweet releaser of endomorphins,
how dare they speak of sin
when addressing

the descendants of Theobroma Cacao,
the divine barbaric pod

that makes every mouth a god?

Light Up Your Pipes

Like me, this pipe so fragrant burning
Is made of naught but earth and clay.
To Earth I too shall be returning.
It falls and ere I'd think to say
It breaks in two before my eyes.
In store for me a like fate lies.
On land, on sea, at home, abroad
I smoke my pipe and worship God.

JOHANN SEBASTIAN BACH

Clay thou art
and unto clay
thou shalt return.

So smokers
of the world
unite.

Light up your pipes
at break of day
and fall of night,

Send up your smoke
in swirling fugues
to heaven's door.

Intoxicate
the gods
with a frail

crescendo
of mortality.

Coffee in Heaven

You'll be greeted
by a nice cup of coffee
when you get to heaven
and strains of angelic harmony.

But wouldn't you be devastated
if they only serve decaffeinated
while from the percolators of hell

your soul was assaulted
by Satan's fresh espresso smell?

Lucifer to the Patriarch

Before I SUE
the BIBLE
for LIBEL
against female ISSUE

I'll trace
the TESTES
in the TESTAMENTS
and won't let the MENSES
           go unsung.

I'll kiss
the red LIPS
of APOCALYPSE
GOSsip with the GOSpel
and sprinkle witch hazel
           in my sabBATH

I'll exalt
the CAT
in Mary's MAGNIFICAT
join the COVEN
in your COVENANT
and put a bun
           inside my OVEN

I'll set fire
to the PARSON
stand accused
of ARSON
and from the PULPIT
So be it
PULP a sermon
           on my MOUNT

And before all hath
        come to pass
           I'll FEAST instead of FAST.

Suspicion About the Wind

It is my sneaking suspicion
that the wind has big buttocks

When rocks wear away you blame erosion
when time takes a toll of hillsides
when roots strain and land slides
again you blame erosion, geological shocks,
the slow corroding hand of water

But it is my sneaking suspicion
that it's the wind, the tired wind,
resting those ample buttocks
on hilltops on treetops on mountaintops
anywhere grand and accommodating

And when the wind farts, heaven help you.

If Only You Knew

Fishnet tights
on cloven feet
may seem effete

and red nail varnish
on ten talons
may seem sort of swish
or even tartish

but bet you'd wish
you hadn't said
slut and slag
if only you knew

it was the devil

in drag.

Istory Lesson

If it is sluttish to drop one's aitches, then Queen Elizabeth I was a slut.
ANTHONY BURGESS: *Signals in the Dark*

If dropping er aitches
turns a queen to a slut
then a slut I shall be.

So send in a gallant
to arness me royal aunches
for I'm feeling orny.

I'll even ave a commoner
if e's ardy in bed.
But touch my maid of onour,

and so elp me God
it's off to the Tower
and good riddance to is ead.

Comrade Luther

Do you really think
you could scare me
with a pot of ink
Comrade Luther

I will pour the grapes
of God's Word
into filthy vessels
Comrade Luther

I will match horns
with your hallowed text
Comrade Luther

I will cast my spell
in the hell of your bowels
Comrade Luther

I will lean on your fart
for my staff
Comrade Luther

I will be the fly
that perches on your stool
Comrade Luther

I will ride you between
the sheets of the Good Book
Comrade Luther

Even if you change
your sex to neuter.

Have a Chickpea on Me, Mahatma Gandhi

Mahatma Gandhi, venerable Babu,
I'd like a word with you.

You who taught the English the virtue
of cotton; the politics of salt;
and the omnipotence of chickpea.

What's all this I hear about you lying half-
dhoti-clad among honey-skinned virgins
to rigidly test your celibacy?

Between you, me and the Raj,
I'm sure you must have been randy
but O so beautiful at camouflage.

Hierarchy of Heels

Imelda Marcos, you made the news
because of 3000 pairs of shoes
laid out neatly as church pews.

Did the Pope give your feet his blessing
on that memorable state visit?
Your taste in shoes was certainly Catholic.

I'm only asking because I'm nosey.
And I'd like to canonise your toesy.

The Elephant Man

Say Joseph Merrick from Leicester
and the name may not ring a bell.
But say the Elephant Man
and there'll be a tale to tell –

The crowd-puller at the freak show.
The one whose fortune was his face.
The one with the god-like grimace
and an elephant's inward-looking grace.

You who only ventured out at night.
On whose face deformity flowered.
Women, they say, fainted at your sight.
But the rose of your spirit soared upward.

Head filled with the Bible and Jane Austen,
Walk on, Merrick, towards your heart's heroine.
And in the eye of the beholder
Ugliness shall trumpet its parables.

Redness of Rose

In the rose there is no shadow, except what is composed of colours.
JOHN RUSKIN

Redness of rose
to charm away
the bleed of nose

Redness of rose
steeped in wine
to make a lover thine

Redness of rose
whose arrows pierced
a nightingale's heart

Redness of rose
on whose petals
Golgotha's blood still falls.

Dearest of red
for whom many have bled
you don't fool me

I saw you blush
that Eden morning
with Eve's sweetbruising mouth

And from your spiral zero
mortality cast
its fragrant shadow

Ask one
who climbed
a ladder of thorns

Ask me, ah Ruskin, long gone.

In the Name of Wu

When a former Chinese concubine succeeded to the throne of the Tang dynasty as the Empress Wu, she struck a note for feminism in more than political terms. Not only was she was the first woman ever to gain the imperial throne by her own machinations, she was also the first to institute the practice of official cunnilingus. Insisting that all her government official and visiting dignitaries paid homage by 'licking of the lotusstamen', she would raise her gown whenever an official visitor appeared to permit him access to her imperial private parts.

DR ROBIN SMITH: *The Encyclopaedia of Sexual Trivia*

Bravo to you, Empress Wu,
who brought a concubine's charisma
to the political arena.

Praise be your name, Empress Wu,
who granted official status
to the art of cunnilingus.

Honour be thine, Empress Wu,
who insisted that pudenda
be part of the agenda.

Hear me, ye future women leaders,
it's time you learnt a thing or two
from this Tang lady Wu.

Ah Golda Meir, ah Indira Gandhi, ah Maggie Thatcher,
what an opportunity you've missed.
You could have addressed male heads of state like this:

> Before we turn to the Middle East
> population control or the European ecu:
> Kneel down, gentlemen, in the name of Wu.

> and without further ado,
> now that the pubis has been kissed
> let us proceed to global crisis.

The Devil's Advice to Old Couplers

So what if his prick
can no longer raise its senile
head. Whisper something vile
into his octogenarian ear
to tinkle the glass of his spine.

So what if her bosom
has now lowered its flag.
Her mind still basks in talk of shag.
And you can at least salute
her with your shrivelled root.

Come all ye couplers.
Now the curtain is drawn
set fire to your autumnal straws.
Frolic among a haystack of wrinkles.
Seize time by the crotch.
Make the Grim Reaper blush.

Or must I repeat in those doting ears of thine
that Sara at ninety saw pregnancy signs
and Abraham at ninety-nine was circumcised?

A FIEND OF THE ARTS

The songs of the poets are the food of demons.

JEROME

*There is no true work of art in which the
collaboration of the Devil is not present.*

ANDRÉ GIDE

*No devil can compel me to write only
cadences of such a kind.*

BEETHOVEN

Artist's Model

Now turn from your newspaper, friend.
whether couched in art or legend
by a black hand or a white,
look for the one with head of horns
– that mastermind of human plight.
But it's time I set the record right.

Look towards the holy grotesqueries
of your cathedral gargoyles
and the margins of your breviaries
delicately drawn with devilries
as if you could marginalise
the revelries of so-called sin.
Well, take it from me, art or no art,
I'm central to the scheme of things.
The masterpiece displayed
on the canvas of the heart.
And do you know I've been portrayed
more often than my rival model: God

Without wanting to sound immodest
I've given artists little rest.
Even Goya who painted bleeding Christ
thought horns also deserved the limelight.
Not to mention Hieronymous Bosch
(H.B. to intimates like me)
whose imagery makes me say 'Gosh,
such divinity, such devilry!'
And goatish features well-hung in a gallery
seem so photogenic so contemporary.
The Muse that answers to the name of Devil
has inspired pen and brush and chisel.
I've even watched myself on video.
But my profile looks best in soft medieval glow.

Mona Lisa You Teaser

So you once heard the Pope pray for a pizza?
So da Vinci's fly was open unknown to the geezer?
Come on, share the joke Mona Lisa.
What's the mischief beneath the madonna?

Even the cognoscenti stand and stare
clueless as to her lips' enigma.
If only they knew her thoughts: 'Mama Mia
I feel divine with no underwear.'

Impresario Lucifer

If I had my wicked way
I'd have Milton and Beethoven
exchange places for a day

Beethoven, now blind, no longer deaf,
cannot see the orchestra
but explodes into rapture
O heavenly shadows of the maestro

Milton, now deaf, no longer blind,
cannot hear his heroics declaimed
but is almost in tears
O silent lines of satanic flame

Beethoven autographs his *Pastoral* for Milton.
Milton can't find a copy of his *Paradise Lost*.
He signs the sonnet to his blindness.
They promise to stay in touch. Exchange addresses.

I'm glad I arranged this gig in homage to the senses.

A Little Night Music in Mozart's Left Ear

And when the time had come to apportion his ears between us
I said God you take Mozart's right, I'll take the left

and God whispered words like restraint and rectitude
and I Devil whispered words like abandon and amplitude

and in the temple of the human ear
demonic bells rang out their *sanctus sanctus sanctus.*

Devil Diva

Tonight I'll rock
the boat.
Invite Beelzebub
to my throat.
Play havoc
with bel canto.
Screw fortissimo.

Tonight I'll let
my hormones
have the last word.
Time for the crone
to take over.
The high notes
can go to hell.

And as for them
bleeding roses –
they can stick 'em
up their arias.
And if they insist
then they can kiss
my coloraturas.

Dance For Me Brother Nero

What a loss I shall be to the arts.
EMPEROR NERO, 37-68 AD

Dance for me, Brother Nero.
Whirl your pyrrhic torso
across the bacchanal of centuries.

Let taxes wait their turn.
Sit back and clear your throat with poetry.
Wiggle your toes to pantomimi.

So what if Jupiter
hurls down thunderbolt wrath upon your head?
You can always take the *Golden Ass* to bed.

Leave matters of Sword
to your body of advisors.
Arm yourself with librettos and lyres.

So what if Rome burns?
Send in those choral girls
to render their thespian parts.

O what a loss, what a loss to the arts.

Lucifer Relaxes with a Michael Jackson Video

Cosmetic white
has claimed
your black nose

But I'll reclaim
you, cat-son
of cosmic night.

So strike your pose.
I'll lay no blame
at your door

moonwalking one
who seeks childhood's
lost galaxy

among Disney demons.
And when the time comes
for angels to cast

their shadows
among the glittering
abyss of human kind

I'll be there to welcome
love's fallen icon.
Dance on cat-son

On the Flames of Your Strings, Paganini

Paganini, my son,
Take up your violin.
Let music be your sin.

Unravel from your heart
one diabolical note
of human sorrow.

May this one note vibrate
from the roots of your hair
to the tip of your bow.

Climb the ascents of despair.
Be filled with cosmic ache.
Fly on the wings of weeping.

Remember, you are not alone.
Look over your shoulder
into the eyes of ecstasy.

And I promise you, Paganini,
Angels will begin to tremble
on the flames of your strings.

Diabologue

DESCARTES: Cogito Ergo Sum

DEVIL: Copulo Ergo Sum

MOZART: I write as the sow piddles

DEVIL: I kiss as the goat nibbles

MILTON: Better to reign in hell than serve in heaven

DEVIL: Better to reign on earth than serve in heaven

LUKE: For behold, the kingdom of heaven is within you

DEVIL: For behold, the kingdom of hell is within you

BLAKE: The lust of the goat is the bounty of God

DEVIL: Well said, you old sod

The Devil's Poetry Workshop

Mihi nunquam spiritus   *Never hath the spirit of*
poetrie datur,   *Poetry descended*
nisi prius fuerit   *Till with food and drink my lean*
venter bene satur   *Belly was distended*

THE ARCHPOET (*died c.*1165)

The poems I write
have perfect table manners

My poems hold
the fork in the left
the knife in the right

And when my poems
wish to fart
they always say excuse me
in the name of Art

Women Poets Hath No Beard

No beard graced her chin
No hoary growth of Merlin.

No trace of Tennyson's laureate tuft
or Whitman's wildly bardic brush.

No Longfellow's patriarchal halo
or Tagore's sagefully trailing snow.

What? No Shakespearean bristle
or at least a Lawrentian thistle?

Yet her face, unstubbled smooth
seemed somehow troubled by the Muse.

Dear Reader, you are forgiven
for thinking she keeps her beard hidden.

In some private Chaucerian place
where even metaphors embrace.

Lucifer to Holland Day, the photographer who starved himself for a year in order to pose as the crucified Saviour

The Crucifixion
in soft focus.

A Galilean head
overgrown with thorns.

Redemption of sin
mise en scène.
Golgotha framed.

An impressionistic nail
punctuating the feet.

A photographer's dream
or the penance
of an aesthete?

And all that fasting.

I could have saved
you the trouble, brother.
Spared your body
the self-denying test.

What if I told you
I have seen a Christ
fatter than an act
of human kindness.

In the Afterworld of Publishing

Take heart, ye wielders of the quill.
Ye pushers of biro and pencil.
Ye lap-top Sapphos and word-processing Virgils.

In imaginary heaven you shall have your fill
     of paper and booze,
     and at the flick of a finger
      the Muse
shall arrive like a tireless waiter
with a tray of poems, novels, belles lettres et cetera.

And in real hell, where halos are commissioned
     those publishers and critics
     shall stand before the seat of
Judgement
to give account of rejected manuscripts
and uncharitable reviews.
And behold, the truth of royalty statements
     shall be disclosed
     and the bad news
     O Publishers
is that every unearned balance
shall be multiplied like the five loaves.

     But hearken to the good news,
     O Authors
In the hellraising garrets of paradise
     all those who write
     shall throw down their pens and
dance

Lucifer Addresses Hollywood's Oscar Ceremony

Hysteria, gothic as Dracula,
has cast its cinematic stigmata
on the celluloid imagination
of the Big Apple nation.

In my humble opinion, Hollywood
has spread its doctrine of jolly blood
to farthest corners of the universe.
A neo-empire of the Werewolf's curse.

Even where poverty tightens its vice,
vampires in bikinis and gory gigolos
have conquered New World screens and videos.

A bleeding orifice makes good box office
and popcorn goes well with porn and terror.
Poverty viewed in a sensational mirror.

However, I'm pleased to present this Oscar
to a rising diabolical star.

Ladies and Gentlemen: The Human Heart.

NEWSPEAK DEVILSPEAK

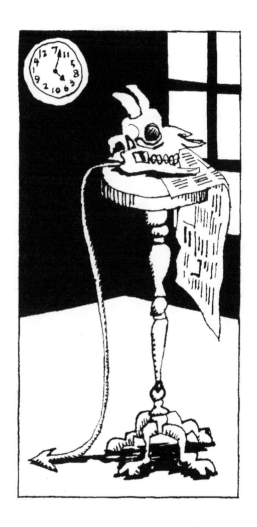

Speech is a beautiful net
in which souls are caught.

FAR EASTERN PROVERB

The Devil's Plenary Address to a Conference on Pre-Millennial Grammar

> *Grammar is a sine qua non of language, placing its demons in*
> *the light of sense, sentencing them to the plight of prose.*
>
> KAREN ELIZABETH GORDON:
> *The Deluxe Transitive Vampire:*
> *The Ultimate Handbook of Grammar for*
> *the Innocent, the Eager, and the Doomed*

I *The Private Parts of Speech*

Let's say the lips
are inverted commas
framing 'direct speech'.

Let's say the ears
are eternal question marks
announcing the abyss.

Let's say the eyes
are fragrant full-stops
at the end of a life's sentence.

Let's say the buttocks
are a pair of open brackets
enclosing an aside.

Let's say the prick
is an exclamation mark
stressing an ejaculation.

Let's say the slit
is a holy hyphen
uniting opposites.

The unassuming rivers of conjunction
that join the banks of your bodies. –

The liaisons of prepositions
that propel you within
    without below between beyond. –

The temptation of verbs
that denote your doing and undoing. –

The fall of infinitives
that split you from the infinite.

The intensiveness of pronouns
that bear witness to the solitary
    stress of *yourself.*

The possessiveness of adjectives
that emphasise the *his* and the *her.*

The persistence of interrogatives
that hurl their questions
    at the *who* and *why* of heaven's void.

But may every adverb be enchantingly invoked
in the name of poetry and song
    to aid your never-ending quest

for a blessed common noun.

Iron

Thou shalt break them with a rod of iron
PSALMS 2. 11-12

If iron be a sign
of divinity
to ward off evil –

of what was made the crusade sword
that laid low the fallen horde?
And should I name again
the umbilical chain
that bound millions to the gloom
of slavery's womb?
Not to mention those tell-tale nails
that stigmatised the crucified one.

Iron –
icon of protection –
god or demon?

Whose side are you on?

Maggie of Assisi on the Steps of 10 Downing

Where there is discord let me travel Concorde;
where milk is laid in the mouths of primary toddlers
let me lay to rest such largesse and bother;
where miners raise their voice in darkness
let me cripple their unison with metropolitan light;
where sheep are invaded, let us rejoice
at the slaughter of shepherds for it is our right.

O Divine Master, grant that I, Iron Mistress,
may not so much seek
to thatch as to be detached;
to U-turn as to upturn;
to stand up as to stand down;
for it is a funny old world
and it is in standing down
that history will stand us up
to eternal life.

Barbed Wire

Barbed wire, your thorns bear
no redeeming heart or rose –
only a desperate bloom
already become living shadows.

And through time's twisted telescope
I see guardian angels
in goose-stepping boots
and a Greek chorus of Greenham women
nurturing the stubborn flame
of hope.

O Cassandra, be my comforter,
feed me plums of gloom
that I may read history's hidden thoughts.

Barbed wire, another name
for you is 'Devil's Rope'.
Yet in your thorned presence
even demons are impressed

by the hand that could fashion
so silent a witness
to the choreography of the doomed.

Anything You Moo May Be Used in Evidence Against You

As in the Book of Exodus
oxen were stoned to death

As in France
medieval pigs were publicly flogged
for breaking the law

As in Portugal
a horse was tortured to confess
and finally burnt at the stake

As in Switzerland
a fifteenth-century cockerel
was likewise burnt as an infidel
for laying an egg

As in Italy
caterpillars were summoned to court

So in twentieth-century Britain
will the cows be put on trial
for the spread of sorcery

Only this time
spare the beasts

Slaughter the mortals
who fed them offal.

Cabinet Reshuffle

Time to reshuffle the Cabinet.
So gather round, my minions, for some tips.

Beelzebub, you brew up the budget.
First, master the art of passing the buck.
Rebuild Paradise on lottery luck.
Remember, misquoting the Good Book
is one way to deal with deficit,
for the rich shall be among you always
and Karl Marx shall have a roll-up in his grave.

Mephistopheles, stay with culture, my son.
Play the maestro with an axe for your baton.
When necessary, demolish a library,
for the end multiplies the means.
Consider in its place a video shop,
tastefully furnished with saintly pews,
so all and sundry can genuflect to the gory,
for there is a time to subsidise the Muse
and a time for giving the Muse the chop.

Pan, take agriculture by the horns.
Farming policies must be reformed.
Replace those sane cows with mad goats.
Rid the fields of cudchewing Buddhas
fit only for fashionable leather.
Let the milk of satyric udders
be delivered at the clink of dawn,
and the proverbial pint shall reach new heights.

Leviathan, sort out the environment.
Don't let a little thing like a forest
stand in the way of Armageddon's target.
Roll up the seas shimmering carpet
for the coming of the harpoon.
Heed not the voices that protest in tunnels.
Think big. Think privatisation of the moon.

Old Nick, jolly red-suited Old Nick,
you're just the kind of fellow
to make a curriculum tick.
With your Santa hat and hearty ho-ho
you're made for the education portfolio.
Who was it that said catch them young?
Start with a classic rhyme or slogan.
Down the chimney, through the crack,
another sinner in the sack.

Lilith, you're no token woman,
though the health services shall fall
under your administration.
Let the sick try the unmissionary position.
Distribute hearing aids to the deaf
that all may hear the howling of the undressed.
Burn all condoms at a public stake
so flesh shall quiver for flesh
and quake at the consequences.

I shall of course keep my post of Chief Whip,
for let each of you remember:
Spare the birch and spoil the minister.

Launcelot and Sublime Brown

It's the talk of the town,
Sir Launcelot has sinned
with a hooker named
Sublime Brown

No wizardry of Merlin
can undo that night
when a dark rose flamed
on a stem of white

Spread the news to Avalon
Speak no word of right and wrong
Say only that the raven
is playing with the swan

A knight of shining reputation
the favoured of the kingdom
caught with his armour down
in the arms of Sublime Brown

I tell this tale of tabloid grail
to young gallants everywhere
who leave behind their Guinevere
to taste the fruit of night

Tis said the blacker the berry
the sweeter the juice
As bards will have their dark lady
Grant Launcelot his chocolate muse

So ride on sons of chivalry
Ride the riddle of your quest
When temptation sounds its sublime horn
Like Launcelot, lay your sword to rest.

I Pity You Your Clocks

Those tick-tock
sovereigns
that cast
you mortals
the meagre
crumbs
of seconds
from eternity's
inexhaustible
table
But what
can you do
when time
cuckolds you
with the cry
of cuckoo

The Devil's Solipsism

BETWEEN THE DEVIL AND THE DEEP BLUE SEA
OR BETWEEN GOD AND THE DEEP BLUE SKY
IT'S A MATTER OF RELATIVITY
OR THE MOTE OF DOGMA IN YOUR EYE

The Real Thing

I

Beneath the moon's crater cradled with possibility
(believe it or not) upon a godcajoling whim
they buried a copy of the Bible in microfilm.
Meanwhile, I clutched my copy of the fairy-tales of Grimm.

II

Leave the earth deflowered
Leave the land detreed
Head for the moon's surface
Plant a coca-cola seed
O new thirst of human breed

III

And the moon's own side a flag shall pierce –
a fluttering strip of cloth
that could hardly bear the weight of a woman's monthly bleed

Millennium Bug

The bug threatens a domino-effect global collapse of computer systems at midnight on 31 December 1999. Designed in the sixties with a two-digit number representing the day, month and year, computers are unable to recognise a change of century which requires four digits. Thus at the turn of the year 2000, the new century will be 00, which computers will understand as 1900. And the fear is it could lead to Mad Max-type Armageddon.

DAVID ATKINSON,
The Big Issue, 20-26 May 1996

What do they expect when they heed not
   the dance of numbers?

Blunders and bloomers
   will be their undoing

bugs will flower in their computers
   for it is written a day will come

when the angel of mayhem
   appears in their IT systems

and demons disguised as digits
   trumpet the collapse of world markets

that trespass on the human soul
   and treat people as dispensable

and the millennium will toll
   its software Armageddon

and zero will be lifted high
   as the laughter of Galileo

and Pythagoras too will erupt
   at the mention of bankrupt

and the Devil alone
   shall sing in praise

   of the counting frame
     and runic rods
     and notched bone

Money Money Money

The filthy rich can afford
to call it filthy lucre
but of course they never do
brooding upon their nest eggs
with the coolness of a cuckoo.
Nor do they speak of 'ill-begotten gains'
or 'the root of all evil'.
And during my own stint in Eden
I never saw a fiver or a dollar bill
hanging from the tree of Good and Evil.
Sure, a fiver in a serpent's tongue
would have looked more stylish than an apple.
Now money talks, but does it hiss,
though I've heard it called the devil's dung.
Ah. The spoor that buys a fragile bliss.

Demon-ocracy

is government
of vampires
by vampires
for vampires

In a demon-ocracy
blood is tax-free
and each member
will have the right
to an equal share.

You are advised
to cast your vote
just after midnight
by placing an X
against your throat.

It's Lottery Time with Mystic Mammon

When the seven numbers have rolled
out the razzmatazz cage
and prosperity grins in gold
from across a tabloid page

then ex will seek out ex
and brother, I tell thee,
will turn against brother
and sisters set at enmity

between parents and children
money's shadow shall creep
and in a king-size bed
the nouveau riche shall not sleep

and you shall rue the day
you rescued that lottery ticket
from an infernal pocket
(all bundled for the washing)

and the washing machine
shall have the last laugh
and there behind the scene
I too shall spare a grin.

Thank You for Giving Me My Due

Devil's Bridge
Devil's Island
Devil's Dyke
Devil's anything you like

Devil's Music
Devil's Sonata
Devil's Trill
Bow maestro to your fiddle's will

Devil's Bones
Devil's Teeth
Devil's Dung
Roll dem dice with devil's luck

Devil's Nostrils
Devil's Canyon
Devil's Throat
Too late now to turn back your boat

Devil's Colours
Devil's Neckerchief
Devil's Livery
How tell he hanged man from the tree

Devil's Bit
Devil's Apple
Devil's Weed
In the night-time sow thy seed

Devil's Dozen
Devil's Candle
Devil's Mass
Who will kiss the devil's arse?

Brother to the Word

I

Where the fine print
conceal its fangs

Where dotted lines
are spoors of deceit

Where language
hides its cloven feet

Where promises
are spoken

with forked tongue
Am I not brother

to the Word?

II

I give you greetings, Christ
Whose salutary silence
upon the Cross
was eloquence incarnate.
But at what cost?

Compañero, I call you Christo
whose sandalled feet
graced Galilee's stones.
Tell the multitude
to leave us alone.

We who divide the Word
like the spoils of a garment.

Valediction to Vulture

Undertaker of the sky –

you who inherit
the kingdom of carrion –
monarch of all you survey.

Why do they defile
your crimson crown
by calling those who prey
upon fledgling innocence
                    'these vultures'?

You are no paedophile
who desecrates the shrine
of childhood.

Here is my valediction
to you, King Vulture.
O archangel of death,
spread your cape of mourning
over this morning's carnage.

Domain of Angels

*...when we wake each morning, we should
check the words in the newspaper as well as
the words in our own mouths. We must treat
words like hand-grenades.*

AMOS OZ:
The Slopes of Lebanon

Go, bombers, to the slopes of Lebanon
for this is a 'war of choice'.
Achieve a result for Zion.

Say 'let us rejoice'
for the Falklands rebels have fallen like lambs

Remember, your enemy may dress the same as you
and even wave your flag.
In which case you'll be a victim of 'friendly fire'.

Lay your dying head upon the desert's lap
for she is the 'mother of battles'

Gather your missiles for a 'pre-emptive strike'
and tell the tidings to a 'task force'

Say Baghdad burns from 'limited collateral damage'
but for a 'new world order' to be established
a few asses must be kicked

O my twentieth-century people, you have come of age.
And if speech is the domain of angels
then who has marvelled your mouths with crooked metaphors
that you cover your crimes in bandages of Babel?

Dunblane

Tell the three wise men of the East
to follow the star to Dunblane.
Evil is about to be born

and once again in human form.

Tell them they'll find no beast with horn
or trail of subtle serpent.
Only the footprints of an ordinary man

who learnt his A for apple like his one plus one.

This journey will not be their first
This journey will not be their last
for through the gates of innocence

Evil has come to pass.

Yet in broken-hearted March
grief pushes out its flowers of spring
and the stones wish they were not speechless

Among the Multitudes for Mandela

O royal ones
let down your crown.
Bishops all
put on your tutus
and dance among the multitudes

for one you called
a terrorist
now walks Redeemertall
among your midst
and Buckingham bows
to Africa's son.

Sound the bells of St Paul's.
Lay out the red carpet.
Scatter his path
with flowers of forgetfulness.
Gather voices
in unison.
Make a mandala
of your hands.
Join Brixton
to Trafalgar Square
where stands
that pigeon-medalled admiral
now lorded over
by another Nelson.

O tickle me
with history's
feathertips
ye tabloid scribes
and pharisees
of politics.

Go plant your pens in shovelled earth.

Question Time With the Devil

When cries of heresy
followed women to the final stake
Did the Devil help to stoke the flames?

When webs of ancestry
became nameless cargo in a ship
Did the Devil chart and log the trip?

When walking elegies
were smothered in a womb of gas
Did the Devil supervise the task?

When the desert bloomed with bodies
and the mother of battles wept
Did the Devil count the score of death?

When tribal rivalry
tore the heart out of Rwanda
Did the Devil share in the plunder?

When divided loyalty
likewise made the heart of Ireland bleed
Did the Devil dance a jig and reel?

When Bosnia shed its grief
down the smooth cheeks of a TV screen
Did the Devil have a peaceful sleep?

O what would you do without me to blame?
But was it one with horns and fiendish looks
who pushed the button and wrote the history books?

I give you half a minute to reply.

Progress

The toad's je**wel**
has erupted into venom.

The flowering shrub
has drawn a pilgrimage of slugs.

The split atom
has blossomed into a bomb.

The glinting ore
has grown a constellation of swords.

And the cloned goat
ponders its bearded lookalike

in a blazing mirage of knowledge.

Gift of Forgetting

If memory is a gift of God
then let it be known
that I the Devil bestowed
the gift of forgetting
on mortal kind.
So whenever memory
begins to beat its wing
against your heart's cage
you folks ought to thank me
for the gift of setting free
into oblivion's wide clouds
the bird that feeds upon your wounds
and nests in your rage.
How else would history
repeat itself
and a tortured heart
find a moment's rest?

Bridge Builder

Bridge-builder I am
between the holy and the damned
between the bitter and the sweet
between the chaff and the wheat

Bridge-builder I am
between the goat and the lamb
between the sermon and the sin
between the princess and Rumpelstiltskin

Bridge-builder I am
between the yoni and the lingam
between the darkness and the light
between the left hand and the right

Bridge-builder I am
between the storm and the calm
between the nightmare and the sleeper
between the cradle and the Reaper

Bridge-builder I am
between the hex and the hexagram
between the chalice and the cauldron
between the gospel and the Gorgon

Bridge-builder I am
between the serpent and the wand
between the hunter and the hare
between the curse and the prayer

Bridge-builder I am
between the hanger and the hanged
between the water and the wine
between the pearls and the swine

Bridge-builder I am
between the beast and the human
for who can stop the dance
of eternal balance?